Nature

OXFORD
PRIMARY
art

Norman Binch

Oxford University Press 1994

The countryside

Artists often get ideas for their work from nature.

These paintings show how the natural *landscape* is shaped by people.

These two paintings were painted out of doors very quickly.

The artists did more paintings from these sketches when they got back home.

 Why did they have to paint quickly?

Using your imagination

These pictures show how artists use their *imagination* to make paintings which can seem strange to us.

One of these paintings is about the sea in winter. The other is about war.

 How are they alike?

This artist wants us to see the landscape as if we were in a dream.

Do you paint what you dream about or imagine?

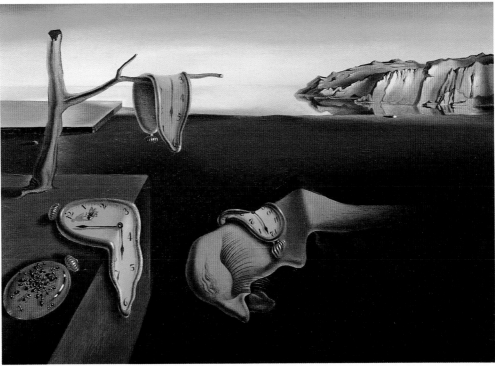

Water

These paintings show us some of the ways that artists paint water.

❓ What do you think has just happened in this painting?

This is a misty river scene. The water is very calm.

These are both paintings of the sea when it is stormy.

 Can you see how the artists have made the sea look rough?

Trees

Artists often make paintings of trees. They also use them to get ideas for decoration.
The wood from trees is used for making *furniture* and for *carving*.

This is a photograph of palm trees. Look at the shapes.

❓ Could you paint them?

Look at how the artist has painted the evening sun
on the tree.

? How many different trees can you see on the
dish?

Plants and flowers

We can get lots of ideas for decorating things from plants and flowers. These pictures show how they can be used for decorating *textiles* and *pottery*.

This is a *detail* of the decoration on a bowl.

This picture of a lily was made by sticking pieces of paper on to a *background*. It is called a *collage*.

Animals

Looking at animals gives us lots of ideas for making art and for decorating things. These animals have been *modelled* and then decorated.

The real cat seems to like his new friend!

Look carefully at these models.

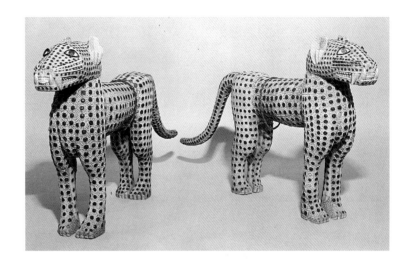

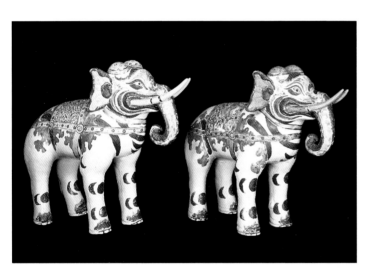

You can make models of animals and decorate them.

Here are some more pictures of animals used in making art. Only one is modelled.

Can you see which it is?

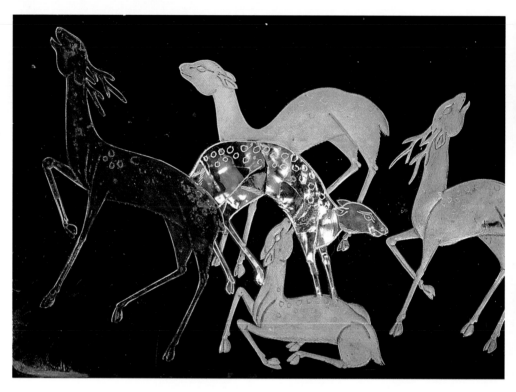

This is a very old brooch. The animal is a 'dragon'.

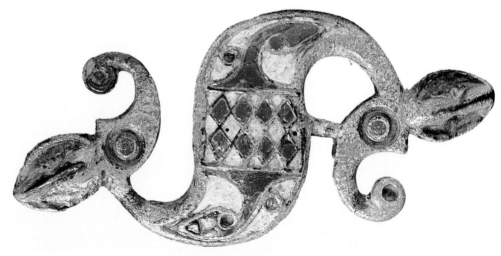

What kind of game do you think the
lion and the antelope are playing?

This is a bed cover with animals and
birds in the trees.

 Can you see them?

Birds

Birds are also favourite *subjects* for artists to paint and model.

This is used for serving soup.

 Can you see the lid?

These are paintings of birds in the landscape and on the sea shore.

This is a *design* for a wallpaper pattern. It would be *repeated* to make a pattern like this:

Birds from Ancient Egypt

These are wall-paintings from ancient Egypt. One is of a man hunting birds in the marshes. The other is of a bird hunting fish.

This is an ancient Egyptian god called Horus. It was like a man but it had a falcon's head.

The four figures below are his sons. They have different heads. Only one is a bird's head.

19

Fish

Fish are also used to get ideas for decoration. You can get ideas for making models too.

Before you use fish to decorate things it is often better to make careful drawings like this.

The dish below shows how a fish can be used for decoration.

Things to do

Make some careful drawings and collect photographs of trees, plants and flowers.

Collect lots of pictures of the sea or countryside and stick them in a scrapbook.

Do some drawings looking out of the window of your house or school.

Try some paintings which tell us what the weather is like or what time of day it is. Can you make a stormy painting?

Get some paper plates or cups and try to decorate them with flowers and plants. Use your drawings and photographs for your ideas.

Try making a *collage* using different kinds of paper to make a picture of flowers or plants.

Make some *patterns* from flower shapes and colours.

Make some models of animals. Try decorating them.

Do some drawings of your pet animals.

Try making drawings and paintings of fish and birds.

Make some patterns using fish or birds.

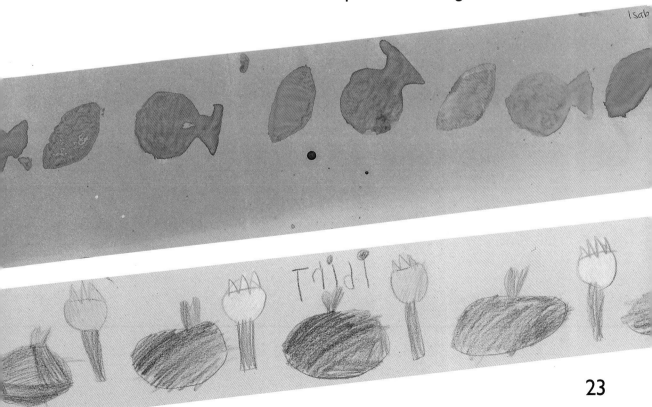

Words to remember

Ideas	Things which come to mind when you are thinking about what to do or make
Landscapes	Pictures of the countryside
Seascapes	Pictures of the sea
Sketch	A drawing done quickly to put an idea down on paper
Imagination	When you think about what something might be like
Furniture	Things in your house like chairs and tables
Patterns	Shapes which are repeated to decorate a surface
Background	Things which are behind something you are looking at
Collage	A picture made by sticking cut or torn paper onto a surface
Subjects	The things artists paint, draw or model
Textiles	Material from which clothes and curtains are made
Detail	A part of a paintings
Design	To plan on paper something you want to make
Carving	When you cut away material (like stone) to end up with a shape you want
Pottery	Cups, bowls, or vases made from fired (heated) clay

Oxford University Press, Walton Street, Oxford OX2 6DP
© Oxford University Press
All rights reserved
First published 1994
ISBN 0 19 834814 2

An acknowledgements list for the pictures in this book appears in the *Teacher's Resource Book*.

Printed in Hong Kong